CHILDREN IN THE MINES
1840 - 42

Compiled and written
by
R. MEURIG EVANS

MUSEUM SCHOOLS SERVICE
NATIONAL MUSEUM OF WALES
CARDIFF
1979
1SBN 0 7200 0023 8

To the children who read this book:

The young children who speak to us in some of the pages of this book lived more than one hundred years ago. In those far-off days it often happened that parents would take their young children to work with them so that the money earned might help to buy food and clothing. There were very few schools that children could attend and most people thought it natural that children should work.

Conditions were so bad that eventually the government decided to find out the facts and so between 1840 and 1842 two Government Inspectors visited the areas in Wales where coal was worked and spoke to many children. During the course of each visit they would make brief notes and these would be written up more fully at the end of the day. Later on, the whole report was presented to Parliament.

This booklet deals only with the evidence given by children under the age of eleven years.

Most of the children who spoke to the Inspectors lived and worked in the mining valleys between the Rhondda valley in Glamorgan and Tredegar in Monmouthshire. In addition, children who worked in two collieries in Pembrokeshire tell us something of their lives. It was in these areas that some of the earliest coal workings were found.

The coal was obtained in one of two ways. The first method made use of a "level." This was a tunnel going into the side of the hill with smaller tunnels leading off from the main one (see Figure 1). Going into one of these levels was just like going into a cave. The second way of getting coal at this time was by digging a shaft and lowering the workers down in some form of container (see Figures 3 and 7).

Although the words spoken by these little children shocked many people then, as it does today, it was very many years before the law forbade the employment of children under fourteen years of age.

A visit to the mining section in the Industry Gallery of the National Museum of Wales, Cardiff, can help you to understand part of the story of coal mining.

Some children worked in the iron industry. Their story is told in another Museum publication, 'Children in the Iron Industry.'

October, 1979.

A photograph of a young collier girl taken a hundred years ago. Under her arm is a metal food box and in her left hand a container for water (examples of these can be seen in the National Museum). This young girl was, perhaps, a little more fortunate than her friends for she had a thick cap to protect her head, warm clothing and a pair of stout boots.

Merthyr Tydfil

Our story is about some of the hundreds of very young children who worked in the coal industry of South Wales more than one hundred and twenty-five years ago. In the Merthyr Tydfil area there were large numbers of workings supplying coal to the four large iron works known as Cyfarthfa, Dowlais, Penydarren and Plymouth works. At the time of which we speak Merthyr was the largest iron producing centre in the world and people flocked from all parts of Britain to the town in the hope that they might make a fortune.

The iron-masters like the Crawshays and the Guests not only owned the iron furnaces and the coal workings, but the hovels in which the people had to live.

Very few children who worked in the pits or the iron works ever had the opportunity of going to school. There were not many schools in existence at this time and in any case parents had to pay if they wished their children to attend. Food could be bought only by earning money and so all who were able-bodied, no matter how young, were expected to work.

It was easy to enter and leave many of the mines because they had no shafts but merely tunnels leading down into the mountain; these were called 'levels'. When they were frightened many of the young children who worked in the mines ran home.

Phillip Phillips was a lad of nine years of age whose face

was very scarred as a result of an explosion at one of the Plymouth mines in Merthyr. Young Phillip was a door keeper. That meant that he had to sit near a door, often in complete darkness, and open and close it when coal was taken along the passage way. These doors were necessary to keep the coal pits reasonably well ventilated and free from poisonous gases. In spite of such precautions, however, serious explosions were common affairs. When he was questioned by the Inspector of Mines, Mr. R. W. Jones, young Phillip said:

'I started work when I was seven. I get very tired sitting in the dark by the door so I go to sleep. Sometimes when I am hungry I run home for some bread and cheese. Nearly a year ago there was an accident and most of us were burned. I was carried home by a man. It hurt very much because all the skin was burnt off my face. I couldn't work for six months. My father is a carpenter. I have seven brothers and sisters but only five of us can find work. None of us have ever been to school.'

A pretty little girl of six years of age, whose name was Mary Davis, also worked in the Plymouth Mines. She, too, was a door keeper. When the Government Inspector came along to talk to her she was fast asleep against a large stone that had been dislodged from the side of the tunnel. After being wakened she said:—

'I went to sleep because my lamp had gone out for want of oil. I was frightened for someone had stolen my bread and cheese. I think it was the rats.'

Figure 1. Here is a drawing made during the last century in which we can see women emerging from a level carrying coal in baskets. Most of these women went barefooted summer and winter. It was from levels like these that children ran home when they were frightened.

Susan Reece, who was also six years of age and a door keeper in the same colliery said:—

'*I have been below six or eight months and I don't like it much. I come here at six in the morning and leave at six at night. When my lamp goes out, or I am hungry, I run home. I haven't been hurt yet.*'

Susan's brother, John Reece, who was eight years old, filled the wagons with coal and he said:—

'*I help my father and I have been working here for twelve months. I carry his tools for him and fill the drams with the coal he has cut or blasted down. I went to school for a few months and learned my a.b.c.*'

Some unfortunate children rolled in their sleep on to the tram lines and were crushed by coal wagons.

Pontypridd area

Maesmawr Colliery was to be found in the valley of the River Taff, south of Pontypridd and was owned by George Insole. In 1840 there were 157 people working in the mine of whom twelve were under 13 years of age. The mine was entered by a shaft which was 60 metres deep. In this mine no children were less than ten years of age and the children employed worked only from eight to ten hours per day. The colliery had a medical fund and everyone had to pay $1\frac{1}{2}$ new pence in the pound towards this. Twelve boys were employed to pump out the water and John Fuge, who was eleven years of age, was one of these.

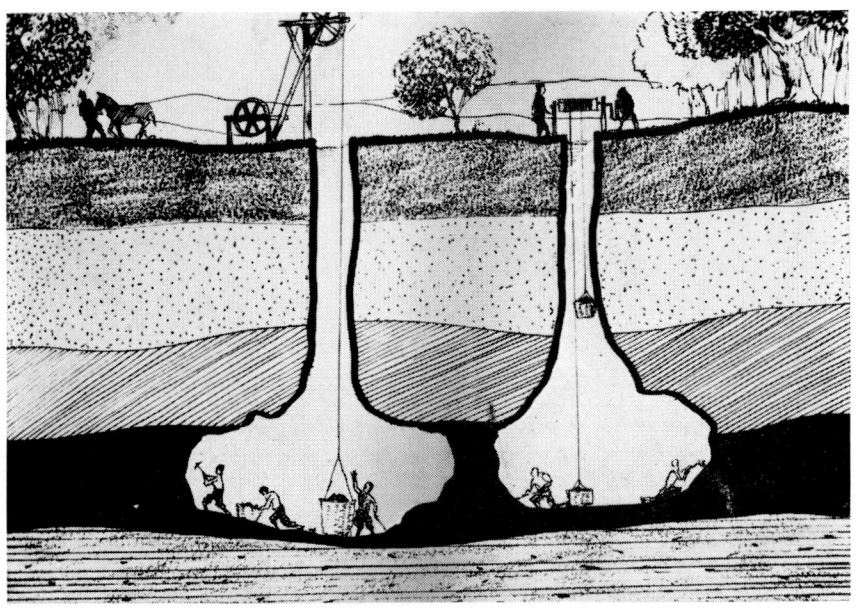

Figure 2. One of the earliest methods of mining coal in the nineteenth century was by means of a 'bell pit', so called because the shaft and hole dug by the colliers was shaped like a bell. In this drawing can be seen two methods of raising coal. On the left is a horse gin; this was simply a rope passing over one wheel and under another and attached to the horse. To raise the basket the horse moved forward and to lower it the horse was backed towards the wheel.

This method was commonly used in Pembrokeshire where a windlass consisted of a wooden drum around which the rope was wound. Teams of women usually operated the windlasses in the pits of Pembrokeshire.

'I started work when I was seven cutting slates in Cornwall. I came to Wales two years ago. This is a very wet mine and once we start work our feet are never dry. It is very hard work on the pumps so we can only work for about eight hours at a time. Sometimes I get so tired that I don't care about eating. When I am thirsty I drink the water in the mine. I earn thirty pence a week and I work every day so I can't go to Sunday School. My father is not very well but when he works he earns eighty pence a week. On Sundays I have bacon and sometimes fresh meat. I have five brothers and sisters.

The Rhondda Valley

The Rhondda valley was once world famous for the excellent quality of its coal and in the latter half of the last century many mines throughout the valley supplied coal to all parts of the globe. Today only two or three collieries are to be found in the valley and the young children who are telling us their stories would hardly recognise present-day mines.

One of the earliest pits in the Rhondda valley was at Dinas and was owned by the famous Walter Coffin.

He claimed in 1840 that he never employed females but he did employ boys as young as eight years of age. This colliery had a small school attached to it and all the workers had to contribute one new penny per week to the fund.

Philip Davies was a boy of ten years of age who was pale

Figure 3.
Before cages were used to raise coal and workers in the pits, a number of different ways were used. Here we see men and boys being brought to the surface. Only men were allowed in the basket; the boys had to cling to the chain or rope to which the basket was attached. It was not unknown for accidents to happen when this method was used.

In many pits ladders would be used for the workers to ascend and descend. There would be a number of these fixed to the side of the shaft and a small platform between each ladder so that a worker who was tired might rest for a few moments before climbing the next stage. Children would cling to the backs of the men when ladders were used in a pit.

and under-nourished in appearance. His clothing was thin and ragged. He could not read. He was in charge of a horse that pulled trams.

'I have been driving horses since I was seven but for one year before that I looked after an air door. I would like to go to school but I am too tired as I work for twelve hours. Every other week I work nights.'

There were very many children like Philip in Wales at this time. During the winter months they would go to work in the dark hours and return home long after daylight had gone. Their homes might be lit by flickering candles and there was little for them to do other than go to bed in a small room which might hold half a dozen or more other members of the family and, quite frequently, lodgers also.

Most children lived their lives without going more than a few miles from their homes. There were stage coaches passing through some of the towns and villages of course but few ordinary people could afford to travel by these. Unlike the workers of today people had no annual holidays; indeed, they considered themselves fortunate if they could have an occasional Sunday free from work.

Figure 4. A drawing showing the bottom of a shaft and a collier arriving after being lowered from above. Baskets of coal are waiting to be hoisted to the surface. The main source of light in the pit was the candle and two can be seen in the drawing, one held by the young boy and the other held by a holder fixed in the roof.

Gelligaer area

Top Hill Colliery employed 67 people. The manager told the Inspector that fewer than five of these could read. He also said that it was easy to tell a collier boy from others as they were *'pale in their looks and thin and weak in their limbs.'* This colliery had no shaft but was entered by a level. Richard Richards was a collier who was seven years of age and worked with his father. He spoke to the Inspector through an interpreter.

'I help to fill my father's coal and sometimes he even lets me cut it in his stall. I work for about ten hours a day and sometimes I get very hungry. I was six when I first came down. I can only speak Welsh.'

When Richard was speaking of his father's stall he was referring to the space in which his father worked cutting coal. (An example of such a stall can be seen in the mining gallery of the National Museum of Wales).

Another colliery in the Parish of Gelligaer was that known as the Llancaiach mine. In this colliery worked a little boy of five years of age, John Davis, who had been taken down by his father. Another young lad, David Harris, who was eight years of age and an air door keeper said:—

'I have been below for two months and I don't like it. I used to go to school and I liked that best. The pit is very cold sometimes and I don't like the dark. I earn three pence a day and I go to Sunday School.'

In the Gilfach Bargoed colliery was a seven year old collier whose name was Ellis Lloyd. He could not read and did not know any letters of the alphabet, reported the Inspector. Ellis said to him:—

'I have been below for twelve months and I get very tired but my father often lets me sleep. I stay down here for twelve or fourteen hours. Father takes my wages and I do not know how much I earn.'

Mynyddislwyn area, Monmouthshire

Between the present-day Maesycymmer and Pontllanfraith there were three collieries, the Buttery Hatch, the Bryn and the Gelligroes. As in most collieries, the workmen here had to buy their own candles for lighting, and gunpowder for blasting, out of their weekly wages.

These particular collieries had their own shops known as 'Company Shops' and the workmen were forced to buy their goods from these. There was a school but few children could go because they were either too tired or they could not afford to lose wages by taking time off. In the Buttery Hatch colliery was one very bright and intelligent young boy of about seven and a half years of age. Attached to his cap was a candle holder and in his button hole was a clay pipe. His name was William Richards. He told the Inspector:—

'I don't know how old I am but I have been down here about three years. When I first came down I couldn't keep my eyes open but now I sit by the door and smoke my pipe. I smoke

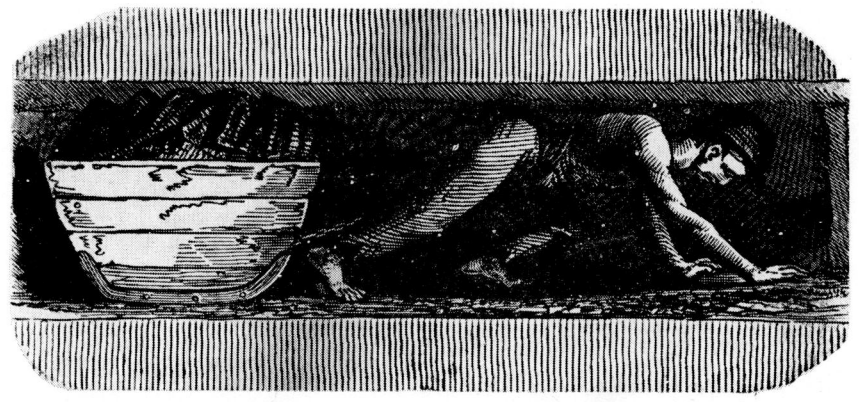

Figure 5. Here is a young boy pulling a sledge on which is a wooden tub full of coal. Around the boy's waist is a harness and from that running down between his legs and attached to the sledge is a chain. Examples of a sledge and a chain and harness can be seen in the Mining Gallery at the National Museum of Wales.

about 2 oz. a week and it costs about two pence. I don't know what tobacco is made of.'

A minister called the Reverend Edward C. Jenkins kept the school near the mine. He had two sons and one of these, who was only seven years of age, was an air door keeper in the same colliery as William Richards. His name was Josiah Jenkins and he said:—

I have been down eighteen months and I get three pence a day. I have not been hurt yet. It is very wet where I work. My father is a preacher and taught me to read a little before I came to work but I have worn it out (forgotten).'

Another little boy in the same colliery was Jeremiah Jeremiah, aged ten, who was a collier and had worked there for five years. His father was dead and he himself had a very disfigured face as a result of being burned in an explosion when he was five years of age.

William Skidmore, who was eight years of age, was another one who worked at Buttery Hatch. His hand had been crushed by a roof fall but he had been able to go back to work after a spell at home.

Young children's duties in the mines

Many young children, as we have seen, were employed as air door openers. A child might have as many as five or six doors to open and he would have to sit, often in the dark, listening for the sound of the approach of trams. The door

List of coal pits mentioned in the story. (See map on next page)

AREA	NAME OF COAL PIT
Merthyr Tydfil:	Plymouth; Dowlais.
Rhondda:	Dinas.
Pontypridd:	Maesmawr.
Gelligaer:	Top Hill; Llancaiach; Gilfach Bargoed.
Mynyddislwyn:	Buttery Hatch; Bryn; Gelligroes.
Briton Ferry:	Esgyrn.
Rhymney:	Evan Jones.
Tredegar:	Tredegar.
Pembrokeshire:	Begelly; Thomas Chapel.

All these pits were entered by means of a level or a shaft. By today most of the evidence that they existed has disappeared.

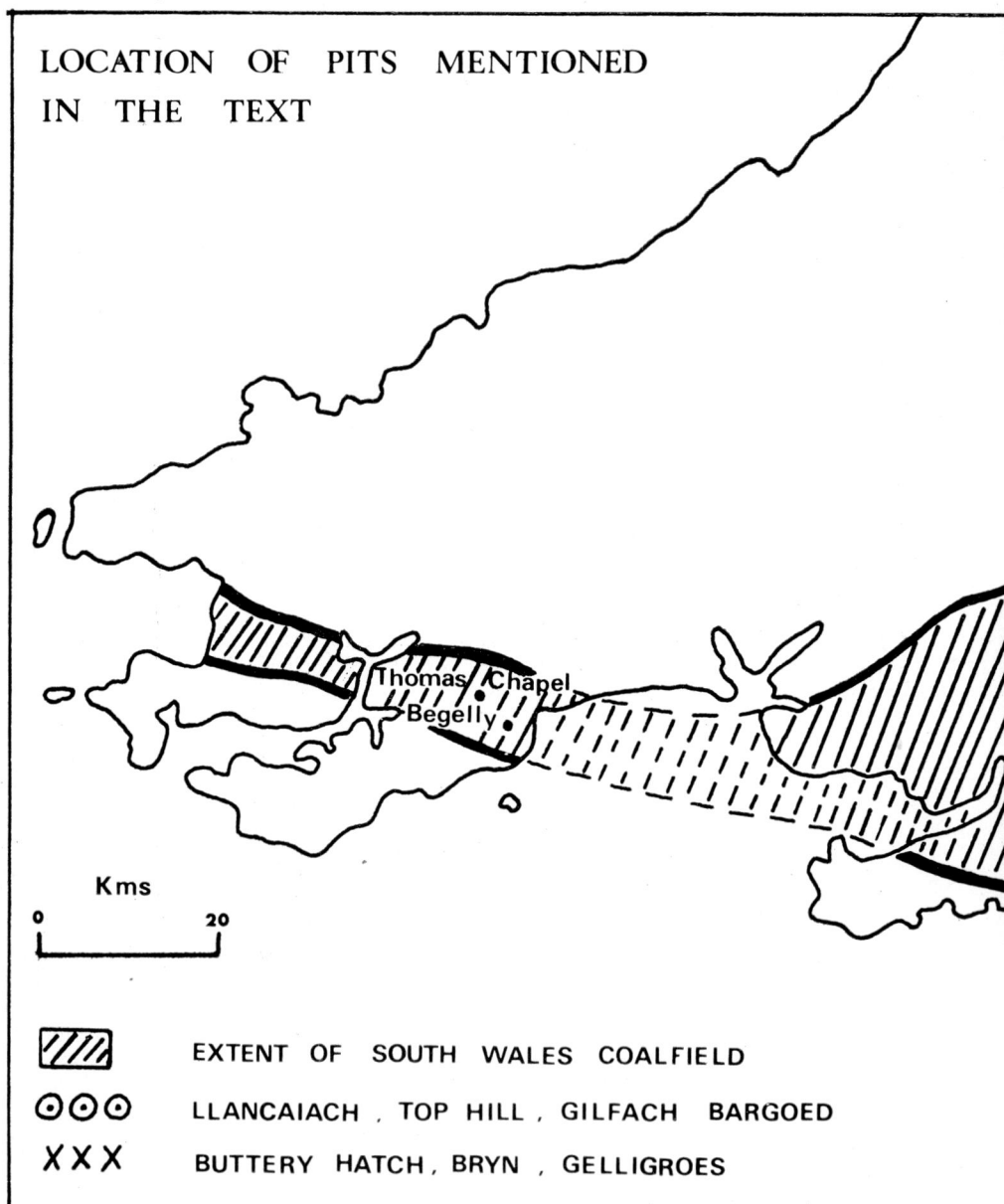

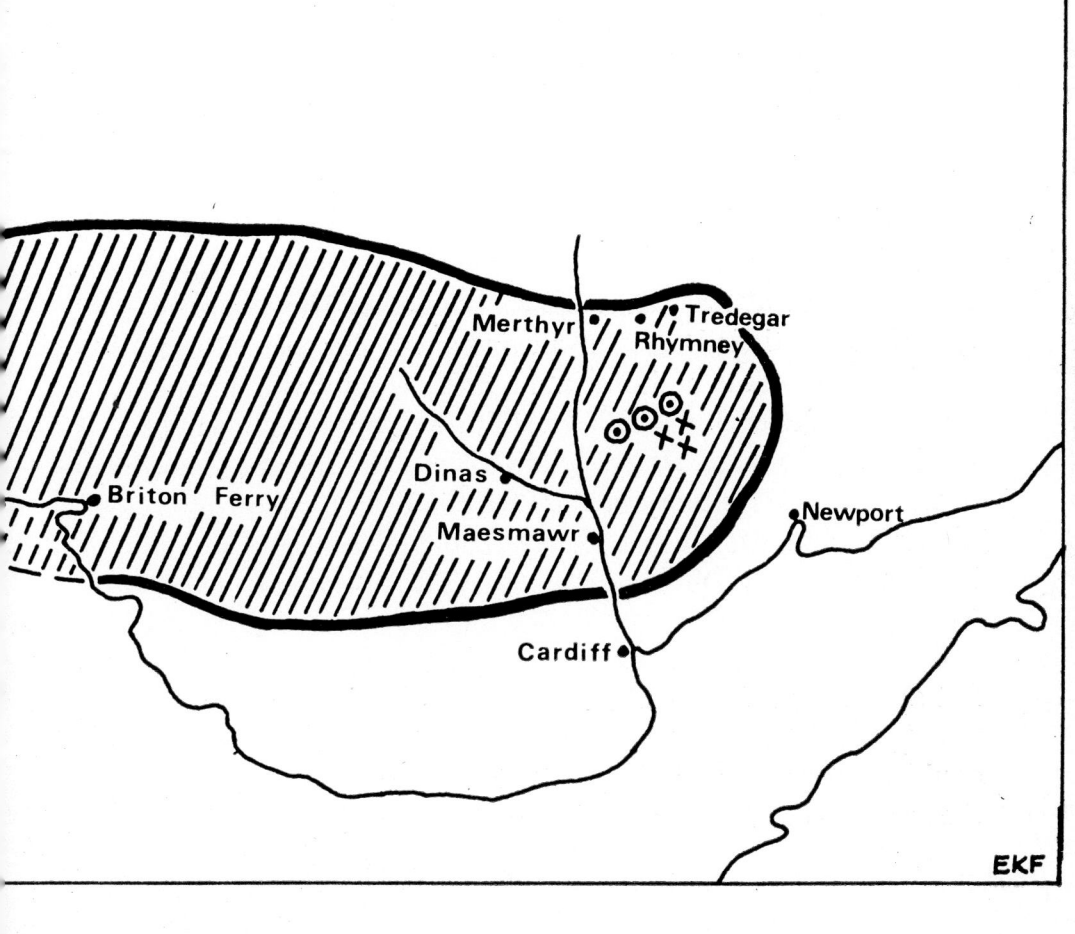

would have to be opened and closed, then he would run ahead and open and close the other doors for which he was responsible. For this the wages were from 2½ new pence to 3 new pence per day.

Carters were boys who hauled the carts or skips of coal from the coal face to the main roadway leading out of the mine. Often the carters could only crawl; around the waist they would have a leather girdle and from this to the cart would be a chain which passed between the legs. (*Figure 5*.) It was very hard work and for a twelve-hour day a boy could expect to get about 45 new pence per week.

On the main roadway leading out of the mine the hauliers would be found with their horses. These hauliers were usually older boys of at least thirteen years of age. They were responsible for their horses at all times and fed them during the day and took them home at night if the mine was entered by means of a level instead of a shaft. Not only the boys but the horses too were always glad to leave the pit at the end of the day. Nearly every boy would climb on to the back of his horse and dash madly away from the entrance to the level towards the field where the horse was pastured.

Children who pulled or pushed trams, when horses were not available, were called trammers. Sometimes these trams merely consisted of containers without wheels. Pulling these could be dangerous work for it was frequently known for the trams to run forward over the unfortunate boy. (*Figure 6*.)

Figure 6. Three young 'trammers' moving coal. The lad on the left is using a harness and chain and his companions are pushing the tram. Trams such as this usually held about five hundredweight of coal. It was rarely possible for even young boys to stand up in the passageways.

Edward Edwards, who was aged nine, was a carter in the Esgyrn Colliery near Briton Ferry and he described how:—

'*I have been working here for three months and I drag carts loaded with coal from the coalface to the main road, a distance of sixty yards. There are no wheels to the carts. It is not so well to drag them as the cart sometimes is pulled on to us and we **get** crushed often. I have often had my fingers and feet hurt and had to stay home for some days.*'

Benjamin Thomas was about eight years old and worked in the Broadmoor Colliery at Begelly in Pembrokeshire hauling skips of coal. The Inspector described him as a 'very pitiful-looking little fellow', and Benjamin tells us that:—

'*I have been working here for twelve months helping my brother to haul skips. I get bacon meat on Sundays but not much meat during the rest of the week. Sometimes I have oatmeal broth before coming to work. The work is very hard and I am running all day. My father is dead and my mother works in the colliery with my sister and three brothers. None of the boys in this pit wears shoes. When I get home I wash my feet and face and play about.*'

We must remember that Benjamin's home was probably a one or two-roomed cottage with a thatched roof. Water would have to be brought from a well and this was another task that the Thomas children had to perform either before or after work, so there was little time for play.

The nearby Thomas Chapel Mine was owned by Thomas Stokes who stated that 'the children generally work two to three hours longer than the adults.' An eight year old boy called James Davies worked in this mine and he said:—

'I have been below one year and I earn ten pence a week which my father takes. I work with my brother, who is eleven, pushing trams. I have never been hurt and I work longer than my father. I have been to Sunday School but never to day school.'

One of James's friends working in the same colliery was a younger boy of seven years of age whose name was David Thomas. When speaking to the Inspector, David said:—

'I am a trammer and I have been working here for four months. I work the same time as James Davies but I work harder so I earn twelve and a half pence every week. I have not been hurt yet. I can't read any letters and I don't go to chapel.'

Most of the children were naturally terrified of being injured at work and expected, sooner or later, to have some form of accident. Both James Davies and David Thomas and many other children proudly told the Inspector that *'I have not been hurt yet'*, but they had been working only a matter of months.

The trams that these two boys pushed in the Thomas Chapel mine ran on wheels but it must be remembered that each tram used here contained seven hundredweight of coal and only two boys were allowed to each tram. No wonder they worked longer hours than the adults, for they were

Figure 7. Here is another view of a windlass. The rope here is merely attached to a log on which a woman sits. Her safety depends on the woman on the handle of the windlass. The darker black bands in the drawing are the galleries where the coal is dug. These are separated by layers of rock. It is easy to imagine how the roof of a gallery might collapse if not supported by strong timbers.

expected to remove all the coal cut by the colliers before the next shift came on duty.

Many more women worked in the mines of Pembrokeshire than elsewhere in Wales. They usually worked in groups of about six, winding the baskets up the shafts loaded with coal, or men and boys. (*Figure 7.*) They were also to be found underground where they used a windlass and rope to pull the trams or skips up a slope. (*Figure 8.*) The men and boys of the Pembrokeshire mines would never consider working on the windlass but always left that task to the women.

It was very rare to find anyone beyond the age of about fifty working in these mines, for the dust affected their lungs so badly as to make them incapable of working. They were referred to as having bad breath, that is, they found difficulty in breathing.

Men could expect to earn about eight new pence per day working a six-day week, while women on the windlasses could expect fifteen new pence per week. The rent on a cottage, usually consisting of two rooms, would be about two pounds a year. Many of the colliers kept a cow and it would find its food by grazing on the verge at the side of the road.

These mines in Pembrokeshire were concerned mainly with producing coal for export in small boats that left from the creeks on the coast and sailed to places like Bristol.

Figure 8. Sometimes windlasses were used underground, particularly to haul tubs of coal up a steep slope. Here again gangs of women operated the windlasses. In Pembrokeshire men would not consider doing this type of work.

Many of the mines in Glamorgan and Monmouthshire produced coal for the iron works that were owned by the same person, and stood close to the mine. This was particularly true in Merthyr, Rhymney, Tredegar and Blaenavon.

It was to such places as these that whole families flocked from the villages in the countryside of Wales in order, they thought, to make huge fortunes before returning. Few, if any, made even enough to buy their own houses and the small number that returned home usually went empty-handed.

How a collier spent his earnings

The Government Inspector in his report tells us something of how the people lived, not only in the pits but also in the few hours they spent between finishing work and going to bed. We are given examples of the wages earned and how these wages were spent.

David Thomas was a collier who lived at Llangennech in Carmarthenshire. He had a wife and four children; two boys aged eleven and four, and two girls aged seven and one. Mr. Thomas earned 70 pence a week; one boy earned 20 pence. So the family earned a total of 90 pence each week.

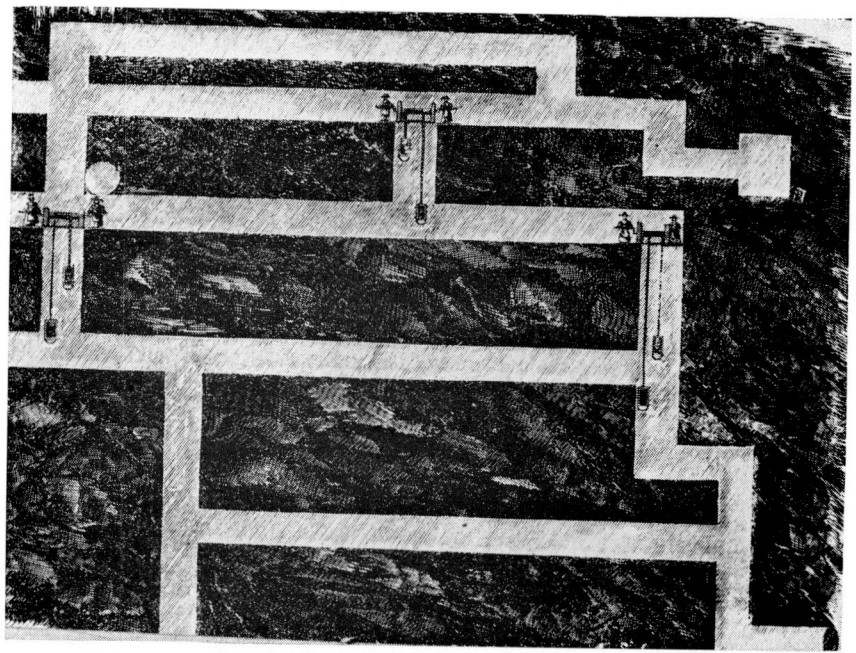

Figure 9. Some pits were operated to considerable depths and one windlass was not enough, so a series of them would be used to go from one level to another. This drawing gives an idea of how a pit might become honeycombed with passages. If the pillars of rock were not supported, then falls would occur; this frequently happened, killing the workers.

This is how the money was spent in one week.

	£	p.
20lbs. flour @ 1p. per lb.		20
20lbs. barley @ ½p. per lb.		10
8lbs. cheese @ 1½p. per lb.		12
1½lbs. butter @ 5p. per lb.		7½
1lb. bacon @ 4p. per lb.		4
1½lbs. sugar @ 3p. per lb.		4½
2oz. tea @ 2½p. per oz.		5
1lb. oatmeal @ 1p. per lb.		1
1lb. soap @ 2½p. per lb.		2½
2½lb. candles @ 3p. per lb.		7½
1oz. blue @ ½p. per oz.		½
Rent		6
Tobacco		3
	£0.83½	

From this account it can be seen that 6½p a week was left for clothes. The Thomas family grew their own potatoes and they were fortunate to receive coal free of charge from the colliery where Mr. Thomas worked. They kept a pig every year and killed it in November so that the money received from the sale of the meat could pay the rent of the cottage and buy new clothes.

Cheese and bread always formed the meal of those working in the pits. On returning home there was usually a meal of vegetables with a little meat sometimes, but this was usually reserved for Sundays.

The Rhymney Ironworks in Monmouthshire had its own coal mines nearby and most of these were entered by means of a level. One of these mines was known as Evan Jones's pit, named after the man who opened it. There was only one little girl working in this pit. Her name was Elizabeth Evans and she was eleven years of age. She was questioned by the Inspector and told him:—

'I keep a door in Evan Jones's pit. I came here a year ago from Llanidloes with my mother, father and three brothers. I used to go to school in Llanidloes and I could read Welsh, but I cannot read much now. Evan Jones is the master of the pit and he pays me two pence a day. I go to work at six in the morning or even earlier and come home at six in the evening. I have met with no accidents, but my father was hurt in the same pit where I am. He broke his arm when the horse pulling the trams ran wild. I was with him at the time. It happened four months ago and he is not well yet. I would rather go to school if I could.'

In most of the mines explosives would be used to remove the coal. This was very dangerous, for the gas that collects underground would ignite, causing terrible burns and very often death. Colliers were nearly always expected to buy their own tools, explosives, candles and other equipment they would need from their own wages. If the colliery had a 'Company Shop' then more often than not the items sold would be very costly.

Henry Phillips and his father worked together at one of

Figure 10. In the early days of coal mining a number of ways were devised to get coal from the depths of the earth. This method was used in Scotland and consisted of a circular wooden staircase; as far as we know this idea was never used in Wales. We should remember that although we are dealing only with children in the pits of Wales, similar conditions existed in the other coalfields in Britain.

the mines supplying the Tredegar Iron Works. Henry was ten years of age:—

'I help my father. I fill the trams with coal and bore holes for blasting. I get ten pence a week. I like to go to work better than school but I have only been to Sunday School. I lost a fortnight a while ago from a stone falling from the roof and cutting my head. We stop working at twelve and take about half an hour to eat. We bring bread and cheese usually.'

Many young children worked with their fathers. In this way more money could be obtained by the father putting his son's name on the tram of coal, so claiming the full allowance. Thomas Rees, aged ten, John Davies, aged nine and William Enoch, aged nine all worked in the Dowlais collieries helping their fathers. They all said that they could not read but that they went to Sunday School. Each one had been in the mine for three years and had started as door boys. They started work at 6 a.m. and finished any time between 5 p.m. and 8 p.m., earning twelve and a half pence a week, out of which they spent two pence each for candles to light their place of work. The three of them were all able to report that they had never been hurt.

In the Dowlais Collieries was a level known as Penyard Pit. One of the young lads who kept an air door in this level was Zelophilad Llewelyn, aged nine. He was fortunate in one way because he had been a pupil at the Dowlais Free School for two years and had learned a little English. This was the school run by the famous Sir John Guest and his wife, Lady Charlotte, who had learned Welsh herself and translated the Mabinogion into English. Zelophilad claimed that he liked his work very much and went on to say:—

'The place by my door is dry, and not very far from where the others work. I eat bread and cheese in the works; I do not often lose my bag of food by the rats, but there are some in the works, and they sometimes steal the bags of bread and cheese.'

At this time (1840-42) the Dowlais Ironworks was the largest in the whole world and needed a great deal of coal in order to provide sufficient heat to produce iron. Consequently, around the works were very small coal levels. Little Morgan Davies, seven years of age, worked in one of these levels as a door boy and had no idea how much he earned. He told the Inspector that he had been away ill for some days with an upset stomach and then went on to say:—

'When I go back to work I take bread and cheese and bread and butter with me and eat it when I want it. I eat it sometimes in the morning and then have none all day. The rats run away with my bag sometimes. I wash myself clean every night before I go to bed. I have often hurt my hands and feet by stones falling on them.'

The amount of money earned depended on the amount of coal produced, so little time was spent eating meals. Indeed, many of them continued to work as they ate, as in the case of Thomas Jenkins, aged ten, and his partner John

Hugh, aged sixteen, who were trammers. Thomas, who did the talking, said:—

'We have no dinner time underground. I eat when I can; in going in with the empty tram I sometimes get into it and eat there and John pushes. He does the same sometimes and I push. We have not many spells of spare time in the works. My father is dead and my mother has seven children. One of these is seven and drives a horse in the little vein. The trammers beat him and the others with a whip when they do not mind to get the coal out for them.'

Cruelty towards children did take place in the mines but very few of the children mentioned it to the Inspectors when they visited the mines. Perhaps they were afraid that they might have been punished or even lost their jobs if they had dared to say too much. Although many children did not like working in the mines they realised that the alternative could well be starvation.

Even after the report had been submitted to the government, many years were to pass before the owners of the mines were forbidden to use child labour.

Now that you have read this little book perhaps you would like more information on coal mining. Here is a list of books written for children and dealing with the coal industry.